ISBN 978-1-331-86599-5
PIBN 10244118

1 MONTH OF
FREE
READING

at

www.ForgottenBooks.com

By purchasing this book you are eligible for one month membership to ForgottenBooks.com, giving you unlimited access to our entire collection of over 700,000 titles via our web site and mobile apps.

To claim your free month visit:

English
Français
Deutsche
Italiano
Español
Português

www.forgottenbooks.com

Mythology Photography **Fiction**
Fishing Christianity **Art** Cooking
Essays Buddhism Freemasonry
Medicine **Biology** Music **Ancient
Egypt** Evolution Carpentry Physics
Dance Geology **Mathematics** Fitness
Shakespeare **Folklore** Yoga Marketing
Confidence Immortality Biographies
Poetry **Psychology** Witchcraft
Electronics Chemistry History **Law**
Accounting **Philosophy** Anthropology
Alchemy Drama Quantum Mechanics
Atheism Sexual Health **Ancient History**
Entrepreneurship Languages Sport
Paleontology Needlework Islam
Metaphysics Investment Archaeology
Parenting Statistics Criminology
Motivational

THE WORKS OF
W. J. DAWSON

THE MAKERS OF MODERN POETRY
Revised American Edition, 8 vo cloth. $1.50 net.

THE MAKERS OF MODERN PROSE
Revised American Edition, 8 vo cloth. $1.50 net.

THE MAKERS OF ENGLISH FICTION
8 vo cloth. $1.50 net.
"A splendid work of insight, sympathy and common sense."—*Boston Times.*

THE FORGOTTEN SECRET
16 mo, art binding. 50 cts. net.
"Opens a new world of thought and feeling."

THE EVANGELISTIC NOTE
A Study of Needs and Methods, together with a Series of Direct Appeals. Cloth. $1.25 net.

THE REPROACH OF CHRIST
Introduction by Newell Dwight Hillis. *Third Edition.* 12 mo cloth. $1.00 net.

THE REDEMPTION OF EDWARD STRAHAN
A Social Story. 12 mo cloth. $1.25. Paper 50 cts.

FLEMING H. REVELL COMPANY
PUBLISHERS

The Forgotten Secret

By
W. J. DAWSON
Author of " The Makers of English Fiction,"
" The Evangelistic Note," etc.

NEW YORK   CHICAGO   TORONTO
Fleming H. Revell Company
LONDON   AND   EDINBURGH

New York: 158 Fifth Avenue
Chicago: 80 Wabash Avenue
Toronto: 27 Richmond Street, W.
London: 21 Paternoster Square
Edinburgh: 100 Princes Street

*This book is inscribed
with the name of
Edward Everett Hale, Junior
with the author's
gratitude and regards*

The Forgotten Secret

I

DO we believe in prayer? It is a strange question to ask in a world which apparently accepts and honours both the habit and practice of prayer. Yet a thinker and scientific observer of the eminence of Sir Oliver Lodge has recently declared prayer to be the Forgotten Secret of the church. It is obvious, therefore, that before we can attempt any answer to the question, we must define with some precision what we really mean by prayer.

Some things about prayer we all believe, and are bound to believe, because they are accepted facts in the order of human life.

Thus, for example, we all know prayer to be a permanent habit and custom of human creatures in all ages of the world. Prayer is a fact in history. All religions are founded on prayer. And strangely enough, as it would seem, when we recollect the claim made by Christianity to the primacy of all religions, the practice of prayer is more evident among peoples who reject Christianity than among those who accept it. As one travels eastward, to those lands which have been the cradle of all existing faiths, the hold which prayer has on the common habit of human life becomes more evident at every step. · From the high towers of cities "half as old as time," the sonorous and sweet voice of the muezzin calls the willing multitude to this act, which is the eloquent witness of things unseen. The camel-driver in the desert, the Lascar sailor on the ship, at the proper moment spreads his carpet, and regardless of curious or scornful eyes, addresses his silent invocation to the heavens.

In a Mohammedan mosque I once witnessed a scene which profoundly moved me. In the pulpit stood the reader of the Koran, and after each sonorous sentence four hundred men bowed their foreheads to the ground, reciting the response; and then followed a thrilling silence, through which throbbed the lingering echo of that solemn litany, as it reverberated round the vast dome, and died upon the porches of the ear. A Roman Catholic priest who witnessed the scene with me, exclaimed, "Surely God in His mercy must have a large place in His kingdom for these men, for He alone could teach them thus to pray." The kingdoms of the world and the glory of them may have been given to the western nations, and we may suspect by whom; but the older kingdom of the simple-hearted still is found among the dreamers of the East. The outward sign of that kingdom, now as ever, is prayer.

Concerning this universal habit of prayer, one thing at least may be said, if prayer has no meaning, and no definite relation to the economy of life, it is quite clearly the most extraordinary delusion that ever possessed the human mind. It **is** as though a man should stand at a telephone whose wire is cut, speaking thousands of messages to an unhearing ear, and inventing replies which have their only origin in his own imagination. The incoherent brain of madness could invent no crazier occupation. Either he who scoffs at prayer or they who practice it are mad,—there is no escape from the dilemma. But it is scarcely possible that immemorial custom has no sanction in experience. Reason itself affirms some intelligent Presence at the other end of the telephone. It is incredible that vast generations of men, and among them the wisest and the best, should have spent their lives talking to their own Echo.

Do we believe in prayer? No doubt many of us do believe in what has been called the subjective influence of prayer, which simply means the sanative or composing or uplifting effect of prayer upon ourselves. "He who rises from his knees a better man, his prayer is answered," is an aphorism which probably represents all that many intelligent and even pious persons are willing to admit as to the use of prayer. How little this amounts to we may judge when we find a physician, who is a complete sceptic of religious truth, insisting on the sanative use of prayer as a means of physical healing. That pain may be soothed, and even arrested by the act of prayer; that some poor creature on the rack of anguish may draw a moment's ease from the sweet voice of some woman praying at his side, and from her cool hands laid on him in outflowing sympathy, is comprehensible enough. But if there be no value in prayer beyond its reflex influence, would it not be easy to find many other means through which the same kind of influence might be exerted? Might not one man say with justice, "Music has the same effect upon me—it composes or uplifts me"; and another claim the same effect from the contemplation of art, and yet another from communion with Nature? Life has fortunately many anodynes for our weariness, many tonics for our self-disgust; is prayer but one among many medicines that man has discovered to heal the mind diseased, and raze the written troubles from the brain? If that be all, clearly prayer needs no explanation, for there is nothing to explain. It contains no mystery. It is not a secret. It is a matter of psychology, a matter even of physiology. It is but one of man's many methods of getting out of himself, that he may draw from an ideal world some strength to enable him to endure the struggle and disillusion of the real.

II

LET us now see then if there is any other definition of prayer which is more satisfactory alike to the reason and the spiritual instinct. Such a definition is not far to seek : it is found in the words of the greatest Master of prayer who ever lived. Here is His definition, than which nothing could be more positive and lucid.

But thou, when thou prayest, enter into thy closet, and when thou hast shut thy door, pray to thy Father which is in secret ; and thy Father, which seeth in secret, shall reward thee openly.

Let us postpone for the moment the details of this definition, and ask what is the broad and general statement which it makes? *It is that prayer is man's actual means of contact and communion with God. Thou* and *thy Father :* the *secret chamber,* and the God who *seeth in secret.* We have all seen in the clear green water of the sea-pools those delicate creatures which children speak of by the common term, "jelly-fish." Inactive, they have little beauty, but as we watch them a sudden prompting seizes them, and they push out a score of exquisite tentacles and filaments, which find a response in elements unseen by us. So when a man truly prays the delicate tentacles of the soul push themselves out, and explore the infinite in search of God. The human soul seeks the Soul of the universe, until it grips, and is gripped by, the living force of God. We apprehend that by which we are apprehended. The Soul of the universe enfolds our soul, and for an instant the life of God flows into our being, enriching and invigorating it. When we use these latter terms of enrichment and invigoration, we admit the reflex influence of prayer; but we claim the positive act also of a real contact with God. And as the questing tentacles in the green sea-water find elements of nutriment invisible to us, so our souls feed on God, and draw into the secret fountains of our own life the force of His divine being. This is prayer as Christ conceived it. He and the Father were one —one in the mystery of contact, communion, spiritual absorption. Prayer is thus the commingling of two personalities : *thou and thy Father :* a conscious contact of my consciousness and God's consciousness ; and these two in the act of prayer become for me the only two abiding realities in the universe.

Prayer, as Christ conceives it, is thus the expression of an inner or concealed life in ourselves. It is one of the commonplaces of human observation that every man and woman has a secret life, an unexplored self, of which the world knows nothing. We often imagine that the lonely people in this world are simply those who, for one reason or another, have been unable to form those social ties which are the common features of social life, but there is a much wider sense in which every human creature is lonely. The real loneliness of men and women is the loneliness of individuality, and this cannot be remedied by any social affinities. It may be modified, no doubt; we may find a friend who understands us, or in married love we may find an intimacy which lifts the burden of the years by sharing it; but in the closest of all human relations there is imperfect contact. Large areas of our nature lie unexplored even to the quest of the tenderest love. Beneath the face that smiles upon us daily with the friendliest confidence lies a whole world of thought and feeling of which we have but the faintest and most fugitive of glimpses, or none at all. For many people language is an embarrassment rather than a means of self-revelation ; they are totally unable to express their real self to another. Men and women often live together in the intimacy of the household for long years, and only once or twice, in some rare moment of emotion, really know each other's hearts. What makes the tragedy of such a situation is that all the time each knows the other worth knowing, and desires a closer knowledge, but gropes in vain to find the clue to intimacy. Does any human creature ever tell another *all* that is in his or her heart? Dare they? Where can we be so sure of comprehension and sympathy that we may venture to unlock the last door of the heart and invite inspection? Of whom among the men or women we know can we be sure that " to know all is to forgive all "? Alas, in the best of us there are hidden motions of the spirit, there are the records of hideous things said or done in past years, there are passages of sordid and sorry capitulation to our worse selves, before which, if they stood revealed, Love itself would flee astonished and affrighted. One only has trodden this earth who knew all, yet forgave all; He "knew what was in man," yet still loved him; with Christ utter knowledge was utter love. And in this infinite capacity for sympathy Christ is indeed God to us, for to know Him is to know the Father also.

III

IT is when we thus put against the lone-liness of the human heart the infinite sympathy of God's heart, that we begin to understand the true nature of prayer. The secret life can reveal itself alone to the Father who seeth in secret. Some of us have perhaps imagined what it would mean to us to have a friend who understood us by sheer intuitive sympathy; one with whom we could sit in sociable silence, saying nothing, and yet certain that the silence drew us nearer together than any speech; and perhaps, in rare instances, we have met such an one, whose nature was, so to speak, tuned into a common rhythm with our own, so that merely to be in the beloved presence was to be mystically consoled and refreshed. It is but rarely, at the best, that this can happen between human creatures, but this mystic relation can and does exist between man and God.

He seeth in secret. The secret pain or shame or love is unveiled to the secret God. When we reach this condition in which our hearts are in rhythm with God's heart, we know what prayer is. It is a condition in which we ask nothing, demand nothing, and even say nothing; we simply lean our tired hearts on God. We give up our secret; we allow God to draw it from us, and are no longer lonely.

To understand prayer, then, we have first of all to rid ourselves of what may be called a mechanical conception of prayer. We constantly speak of answers to prayer, but have we ever taken the trouble to define exactly what we mean by the term? In most instances the term implies a kind of mechanical or mathematic correspondence between the thing desired and the thing granted. Prayer is, of course, solicitation; Christ Himself tells us to *ask* that we may receive. But Christ nowhere tells us that we shall receive precisely the thing which we have asked. "The Father who seeth in secret shall *reward* thee openly," is His word. It is the reward or recompense of prayer on which He lays emphasis —not on a mechanical exactitude of answer. We shall indeed receive something, but it may be something quite different from the thing we expected, something that is more precious, or more requisite to us. And here lies the difference between prayer as it exists in the older religions of the world, and prayer as it is defined in the Christian religion. In the older religions the suppliant seems to be continually saying, "Let *my* will be done"; in the Christian religion we are taught to say, "Let *Thy* will be done." The Christian conception of prayer is not to persuade God to do something for us, but to bring ourselves into such submission to God that He may be able to work in and through us. A very simple illustration may make this clear to us. How is it that the wireless Marconi message finds its way to some particular ship? Under the midnight stars, upon the wide white surges of the ocean, there toss, it may be, a score of ships, yet the Marconigram interprets itself to one ship alone. Why is this? Simply because at the topmast of the one ship there is a tiny apparatus which is tuned into exact accord with the corresponding apparatus from which the message originated. They share a common rhythm, and it is by means of this rhythm that this viewless force, which does not so much as exist for all these other ships, becomes intelligent to this one ship. In the same way the object of all prayer is to establish correspondence with God, and this correspondence is possible only when the common rhythm between man and God is found. Prayer is the effort to bring the human soul into tune with the Infinite.

Hence its chief note is submission, its chief aim is receptivity to God. It is not a mechanical answer we seek, but the inflowing of God's being into ours in whatever fashion may seem best to Him.

It will perhaps do more than anything else to clarify our conception of prayer if we discard the word answer, and replace it with Christ's word *reward*. For, in the human sense, when Christ prayed that the cup might pass from Him, He was not answered, for the cup of anguish was not withdrawn. But Christ was rewarded, and rewarded openly in the strength to endure, in the heroism to die, and in victory over death. When, before the high priest, He witnessed a good confession; when, before Pontius Pilate, he proclaimed in unfaltering accents the reality of His kingship and His kingdom; when, upon the cross, He said, "Father, into Thy hands I commend My spirit," Christ received more than an answer to prayer—something better, and something completer—He received its reward. So when we pray, though we may not get quite what we expected, we do always get back something for our prayer, and what we get is something greater and sweeter, and more adequate than we asked. "God is able to do for us far more abundantly above all that we can ask or think"—and He does it.

It was because Christ knew how imperfect and erroneous were men's common conceptions of prayer, that He was at great pains to instruct the disciples how to pray.

It will surprise any one who reads the Gospels with attention to discover how much of Christ's time was occupied in communicating to the disciples right ideas of prayer. It is evident that they did not understand, and were frequently surprised at the part that prayer had in the Master's life. Perhaps they thought that One so pure as He did not need the constant practice of prayer; or that One on whom the public demands of ministration were so heavy, could ill afford the time spent in prayer. It is so that the active man of affairs often regards prayer. He regards prayer as a sort of inactivity. He is incapable of perceiving that most may be happening to a man when nothing seems to happen. He is apt to measure the impact of a man's life upon others only by visible accomplishment, and to overlook the quieter processes of the spirit which make such accomplishment possible. And in the last result of this way of thinking, such a man often values the influence of a great life only by the tumult it excites, by the fussiness and hurry that accompany it, by its outward energies. In the ordinary church life of to-day this spirit is very manifest. The prayer-meeting, by which I mean the meeting for prayer, and prayer only, has a very subordinate place in the scheme of church life, and in many churches is quite extinct. There is much doing, and many run to and fro, and knowledge is not thereby increased, but there is little praying. And in the lives of Christians the same spirit prevails. Prayer has been crowded out of their lives, as it has been crowded out of the church, by the pressure of restless activities, many of which are genuine activities on behalf of the kingdom of God.

Let us observe then what Christ has to say to busy people on the practice of prayer. For, whatever value we may put, or others may put, on public activity for the kingdom of Christ, of this we may be very sure, " God soon fades out of the life of the man who does not pray." And if our consciousness of God diminishes, we may also be sure that it will not be long before the spiritual energies, which are the source of all our pious activities, will diminish too ; and with them the activities themselves will be atrophied or arrested.

IV

THE first thing on which Christ puts emphasis, is *the art of detachment :* prayer is a very secret and a very sacred thing ; *we must shut the door.* "The world is too much with us" ; therefore we must rid ourselves of the world. I have sometimes stood within one of the great cathedrals of Europe, where everything ministered to the spirit of devotion—the painted window, the soaring arch, the glorious fresco, the subdued and solemn light, the sense of immemorial antiquity—and yet I could not pray. I could not pray for one simple reason—the door was left open, and through that open door there entered the clatter of wheels and feet, the rush of traffic, and the clamour of the market-place. Is it not so with us very often in our hurried and fugitive attempts to establish correspondence with God? We leave the door open, and so "our words fly up, our thoughts remain below." Our plans in life, our schemes of gain, our sordid anxieties and yet more sordid pleasures, are with us while we pray. We give the secret life no real chance of expression, because we have not detached ourselves, and have made little effort to detach ourselves, from our public life. The first law of prayer is then the closed door. And if we interpret this law as it should be interpreted, it means something like this : Shut the door of the heart against intruding worldliness, close the porches of the ear, draw the curtains of the eye, listen for the inmost beating pulse of your own being, let the soul be so quiet that its inmost depth may yield up its secret, retire into the inmost citadel of consciousness—otherwise you cannot pray. It is a deliberate rupture of our connection with outward things that is needed, a withdrawal and detachment from them. When thou prayest, enter into thy closet—a deliberate act of renunciation of things outward—shut the door, and be sure that it is shut.

The reasonableness of this counsel is

manifest. Who is there who needs to be reminded that the most sacred acts of human life always take place behind closed doors? Would it not be a profanation of love if the word that binds two lives together were spoken in public, and a yet greater profanation of sorrow, if the anguish of the heart were uttered to a gaping crowd? We need the closed door for all the great occasions of our love and grief. In all pure love there is an element of timidity, of secrecy—it is hard at all times to speak the confession of our hearts, but it is impossible to do so except in secrecy. The lover seeks some inviolate solitude, he craves the quietness of night, the holy light of stars, the deep silence, secure from all intrusion, in which the very heart-beat of his passion may be heard. Sorrow also becomes articulate only in solitude. We wear a face of stone before the world, we move masked among the crowd, and compose our features to the sad hypocrisy of stoicism; it is only when we are alone that

the mask is thrown aside and our tears
have vent. David must needs go up to
the chamber over the gate, and close the
door before he can let his lips utter the
great cry, "O Absalom, my son, would
God I had died for thee, O Absalom, my
son!" Elisha, when he enters the room
where the dead child lies, shuts the door
upon them twain; he can neither pray nor
heal in public. Jesus also, when He enters
the chamber where the hired mourners
wail around the dead child, must needs
put them all out, before He can speak the
word that recalls the flush of life to the
fair girl's frozen cheek. When the be-
reaved mother goes to the drawer which
holds the toys and ribbons and pitiful
relics of her vanished child, she goes alone;
she moves with the stealth of an innocent
conspirator; even the sound of a step
upon the stair alarms her, so that she
hurriedly locks the drawer upon her treas-
ures, and trembles lest another should spy
upon her grief. In these, and many other

instances, we see how much the closed
door means; we see that it is the symbol
of all that is most sacred in human experience and emotion.

But if for these occasions of our common life we do need, and must have, the
shut door, how much more is it necessary
in the act of prayer? For let us recollect
again what prayer is: it is contact with
God. When we bow the knee in prayer
we seek to speak with God upon matters
far deeper than any that lie in the usual
commerce of our love and grief. The
things we dare not utter into any human
ear, we speak to the Father who is in
secret—who, shall we say, is *in our secret?*
The things we blush to think of, the hidden
impurities and corruptions of our flesh, the
old concealments of unforgotten evil hours,
the imagined but unacted sins of our way-
ward wills, our dallyings with evil, our
silent capitulations to the tyranny of habit;
or, if these sins be not ours, though even
the best know much of them, the silent

apostasies of the spirit, our rooted indifference to good, our ready compliance with wrong, our many acts of cowardice and betrayal, our constant sinkings beneath the standard of our own ideals of duty, our stubborn refusals to realize our best selves; or it may be things that cause us even yet sadder compunction, the memory of unkind words and cruel glances offered to those long dead, our hardness to others, towards whose sin, so like our own, we showed no pity; our obstinate, and it would seem incurable, pharisaism of temper towards the weak and erring, our ungraciousness to those we deem inferior, our neglect of the poor and needy, our foolish pride about ourselves, with all its growth of scorn and impatience of others, all its hardening and corrupting effect on our own natures—these are the matters on which we have to speak to God. These, and also other things, more beautiful to recollect: our desires for purity, so often thwarted, our innocent dreams of holy things which we have carried with us ever since we first knelt at our mother's knee, our timid, humble love for Christ which the soul blushes to articulate—all the softer and purer yearnings of our spirit, which are unknown to all but ourselves— these also we uncover to the eye of God. But we cannot so much as detect these things in ourselves except in the atmosphere of secrecy. While we walk amid the loud and sordid things of life our true selves are hidden from us. The true self, being indeed a private self, claims privacy for its revelation. And so among all the wise words which Jesus has uttered about prayer, there is none so elemental, none that goes so deep, as this: *When thou prayest, enter into thy closet, and shut the door.*

V

TRUE prayer is thus also a very *lonely* thing : is not this also the meaning of Jesus? How often is it said of the Master that He went apart from men, that He was alone, that immediately after great manifestations of His power or occasions of popular applause, He sought the solitude of mountains, feeling in Himself the need of self-examination, of the readjustment of His own soul to the calls of His public life? Jesus is alone in the wilderness, alone in the midnight silence of Olivet, alone in Gethsemane, alone on the Cross. Jesus found that He could realize Himself only in solitude.

But one of the fatal features of our habitual life is that many of us are never alone, and never seek to be alone. There are many men and women who condemn themselves to an almost total absence from themselves. Knock at the heart's door when you will, there is no one at home.

Nay, more; many people almost fear to be alone. Solitude of any kind oppresses them, makes them uneasy, terrifies them; the dying away of friendly voices and familiar footsteps in the distance leaves them miserable.

I have for years tried to teach people, and especially busy people whose lives are passed in cities, that it is necessary even for their mental health that when they go for holidays they should seek not the thronged resorts of fashionable pleasure, but the "haunts of ancient peace"; some place of still waters and green pastures, where they might learn the healing and sanative delights of solitude. For myself, I have never failed through all the years of a laborious life to spend some weeks of each year in places quite remote from men, where I could know

> The silence that is in the starry sky,
> The sleep that is among the lonely hills.

Nor, in all these years, has any day come to me when I have not had some hours of perfect solitude, for without such hours I could not live. These are the hours of all true intellectual and spiritual growth.

Have you ever watched the growth of wheat in spring-time? If you have, you will have observed that it grows fastest in the night. All the violent light of quickening suns, all the rapid, tumultuous passage of spring winds, does less for the growth of the green blade than a single night of quiet star-shine, soft dew, and fruitful silence. The human soul, which Christ Himself once likened to the wheat that falls into the ground, also grows best in the hushed hours of solitude. It seems to me nothing less than tragic that so many men and women do not understand this law, and even hold it in derision. They lavish praise upon the strenuous life, forgetting that the root of every truly strenuous life is solitude They pride themselves on the variety and multiplicity of their activities, living lives of perpetual agitation, in which they take a foolish pride, and not perceiving that all that is finest in themselves is ruined by this vain expenditure of energy. Never quiet enough to hear the still small voice of God, never at home in their own souls to catch the gentle knocking of the Divine Guest upon the door, never truly aware of their own real selves—O, how pitiful a misinterpretation of life is this, how gross a mishandling of their own natures! What wonder that such a life is barren of both high thoughts and deep emotions; that it tends more and more to spend itself on trivialities, becoming at last superficial in its perceptions, artificial in its method, and ignorant of all those elements, or nearly all, which have made life worth living to the wise and great-natured men and women of all the generations.

Professor Edward Everett Hale, in the most interesting account which he has published of his conversion during the mission which I held at Schenectady in November, 1905, has given an explicit statement of the part that prayer played in his experience. I began my mission with an address on prayer, recommending my hearers to seek during the day one hour of perfect solitude, in which they might make for themselves "the experiment of prayer." This counsel Professor Hale acted upon with memorable results to himself. He continued the experiment, not for a single hour, but throughout the week, and as he did so, he began to realize himself, and his real needs. "As the week went on," he writes, "I began to be conscious of a curious change in myself, which I did not and do not now explain. My pleasure in the many interests which made up my life began to diminish and become dull. Instead of desiring to finish up the duties of life to turn to its pleasures, I found that for the time its pleasures had little interest. Art, literature, scholarship, the theatre, the various things that had filled my mind, as well as some others which I need not particularize, lost attraction. Further even, plans, possibilities, ambitions of one sort and another, of which I had a number in hand, no longer interested me. . . . I noticed this loss of interest, and entirely without regret. The attraction of nature held on longer than the rest. I remember one morning looking out of the window at a row of elms which I had for years looked at with delight while dressing, taking particular pleasure in their change of aspect with the changing year. I said to myself, quite consciously, 'I wonder if that is going too,' and before I had finished the sentence I was aware that love of nature had gone with the rest. . . . I felt no especial lack, however; I believe I was conscious of a greater interest." The end of the experiment came when Professor Hale knew that all these things had passed out of his life, to make way for the entrance of Christ. There was left to him " Jesus only." And his final summary is, " By my personal experience I can say that the way to the Cross is through prayer."

No one can miss the essential point in this confession ; it is the realization of self which comes through solitary prayer. For the plain fact is that we do not and cannot know ourselves, nor our real wants, till we are alone. We think we want money, fame, applause, social esteem, and a number of similar things, because we choose to live in the environment where these things count for much ; but it is pure illusion ; we do not really want them because we do not really need them. Our real needs go much deeper ; what we need most is peace, internal harmony, restfulness of spirit, equipoise of soul—all that Christ meant by conscious participation in the kingdom of God and His righteousness. The most common experience in all true conversion is a certain change of values. The things that were much to us become little ; the things of which we had rarely thought become of supreme importance. Just as the seismic wave, passing across a landscape, levels the mountain and exalts the valley, so we become conscious of a changed landscape of life, in which are strange depressions and new elevations, so that the things which were gain to us become loss. Thus Professor Hale finds art, scholarship, literature, and lastly the love of Nature, losing their attraction; they melt out of his life because his life has submitted itself to a higher law of gravitation. It is not that these things are valueless; it is simply that we have given them an exaggerated value, and they now sink into their true proportions. When a friend of Newman's expressed wonder that he should have cast away all the brilliant prizes of life in his renunciation of the Anglican Church, the instant retort was, "It is not difficult. One glimpse of eternity makes everything else look trivial." And it is just this glimpse of eternity which we gain in the loneliness of prayer; we see the greater things of life, and the lesser things sink out of sight.

Make the experiment of prayer, then;

submit yourself to the discipline of loneliness: when thou prayest, enter into thy
closet *and shut the door.* I can conceive
no more wholesome discipline for the energetic man or woman than this deliberate
encounter with the spirit of solitude. Mark
off some hour, or some half hour, of each
busy day as your own, dedicated solely to
the private occasions of the spirit. For
that brief period hold the world at bay;
go to your room as to a shrine; take no
book with you, no humblest task—simply
sit still, or kneel down, and explore your
own heart. Celebrate the sacrament of
silence; it will bring with it on the hands
of viewless priests a meat that the world
knows not of, and it will make audible to
you the still small voice of God that speaks
to us only when *we* are very still. One
such hour, rightly used, will teach you
more of God, and truth, and duty than all
the sages can. It will remain with you as
a consecration and an impulse when you
take up again the vexing tasks of life.

You will be stronger for it, more composed in mind, more certain in aim, sweeter and more patient in temper, and as you walk the thronged roads of life once more, you will bring perfume and purification in your very presence. Let your household, and your children, and your friends know that you keep a Lonely Hour for God in every day, when no interruption is permitted; when even Love must stand without the door and wait; for that hour is sacred to a higher Love, and devoted to a more enduring vision. "I saw a Door opened into heaven," said the Apocalyptic Dreamer; be sure of it that Door of Things Unseen is only opened when the doors of earth are shut.

VI

PRAYER is thus a very *intense* thing, and this is the third law of prayer which we find in these words of Jesus. The closed door, the secret place, the thrilling silence—do not all these suggest intensity—the concentration of heart and will in a definite effort of expression? We cannot pray with a divided mind. Our outward life involves a certain dispersal of power; in prayer we re-collect ourselves. We have to call back the wandering thought, to put restraint upon the fugitive desire, to retire from the alluring superficies of life, and find the centre. Prayer is not a passive but an active state; we *ask*, we *seek*, we *knock*—it is so that Jesus speaks. Jesus Himself prayed, "being in an agony"—and the reason why so many of us find prayer difficult or vain is because there is no agony in our praying. We *say* our prayers, we use some private liturgy of our own in which the same phrases con-

tinually occur, but the cry of the passionate heart which brings the sweat of blood
to the brow is not ours. For we may be
sincere without being earnest, and earnest
without being passionate, and passionate
without being agonized; yet only when
we reach the ultimate of prayer in agony
of spirit do we find its divinest efficacy.
Only then does the Strengthening Angel
visit us.

In one of those strange transcripts of human experience which Professor James has
included in his Gifford Lectures, we have
a striking account of what this agony of
prayer means.

" I fell on my face before the bench, and
tried to pray, and every time I would call
on God, something like a man's hand
would strangle me by choking. I thought
I should surely die if I did not get help,
but just as often as I would pray, that unseen hand was felt at my throat. I made
one final struggle to call on God *with choking and strangling*, and behold, floods of

light and glory passed through my soul, and everything became new."

With choking and strangling : does the phrase seem extravagant, unnatural, out of relation with our sober experience? Yet there are those who have known what it means. Jacob knew, when he went out into the dim night full of satisfied craft and confident of success, to find a viewless antagonist who closed with him beside the brook, who seized him with a clutch of steel, and wrestled with him for his life. Paul knew, when he prayed thrice, with what anguish who can measure, that the thorn in the flesh might depart from him. The kingdom of heaven suffereth violence, and violence is needed for its conquest, because never are the powers of darkness so hostile to us as when we pray. Without metaphor, and in sober truth, an unseen hand, nay a thousand unseen hands, are at our throats when we pray, to choke the prayer out of us. For prayer is not only a shrine, but an arena. God becomes, as it were, our friendly antagonist, refusing Himself to us for our own sakes, that His refusal may quicken our desire for Him. He contests our will that our will may grow strong through contest, until at last we prevail. For this is the key-note of Jacob's great experience beside the brook—he prevailed. He rose lamed, but victorious. The mark of the contest was upon the flesh in the shrunken thigh, as it was upon Jesus in the sweat of blood, but the spirit rose up vindicated. This is He who came not by water alone, but by blood. The hand upon the throat is at last withdrawn, and behold the day breaks, the new name and the new nature are won, the peace of God rests upon the garden, and "floods of light and glory" pour through the triumphant soul, making all things new.

The reader of these words may justly ask the writer if he himself prays thus? Assuredly not always, for that would exceed the capacity of the human. But just as there are exceptional and radiant hours of human love, which give the measure of its depth, so there are episodes of prayer, which set the standard of its meaning. Out of the past years such hours return upon me ; times when my back was to the wall; when I was beaten down into the dust and earthly hopes lay ruined ; when all my life hung tremulous above the sick-bed of a little child ; when another life, dearer than my own, trembled in the balance, and the shadow of death lay upon my house, and in the midnight silence I could almost hear the beating of the black wing of the Destroying Angel—and then I prayed, "being in an agony." Then I prayed, and knew myself mystically consoled, as though God took my bruised life to His bosom, and I rejoiced to

> feel God's greatness
> Flow round my incompleteness,
> Round my restlessness His rest.

To have prayed thus, and prevailed thus, though it be but once in many years, is to believe in prayer forevermore. Earth and heaven may pass away, but surer than the stars, brighter than the sun, shines that hour with its unchanging testimony. For just as you must measure love not by its sober average of emotion, but by its highest tide-mark, by its supreme hour, if you would measure it aright, so prayer must be measured by the occasion when it has meant most to us. Never again does Jacob wrestle with the Angel of The Crisis, nor stand beside the stream which marks the great division of his life, but all his life he "goes the softlier" for that hour's sake; never again, it may be, will it be ours to pluck the life beloved from the cold grip of death, but the memory of our Gethsemane abides with us as an element of faith and strength forever. Once, if it be only once in many years, to have found our God in prayer, is to derive courage for a lifetime; and in those duller hours, when prayer seems vain to us, this Supreme Hour comes back to us, like a prophet with the aureole of conquest on his brow, like an angel with the cup of strengthening wine for our faintness and fatigue.

VII

THE great episodes of prayer come rarely ; but nevertheless the habit of prayer should be normal. It should be as natural a thing for the soul to talk with God as for the child to utter without restraint his expressions of affection, his curious enquiries, or his little troubles, into the ear of his parent. There are households where the law of restraint or etiquette is so strict that children grow up in an atmosphere of repression, never displaying their real selves or uttering their real emotions. But in the true household such restraint is unknown. The child is encouraged to be natural, to speak wisely or foolishly as he will, being sure of loving comprehension. In all true intimacy there must be room for foolishness ; indeed how much of all true love consists, so far as its intercourse is concerned, in the utterance of what the world would call foolish nothings, the implicit understanding being that it is wiser to be frank and foolish, than correctly proper and not frank in the exhibition of our feelings. Perfect frankness is the root of all intimacy, the sense that we need practice in the presences we love none of that social deceit to which we instinctively resort when we move among strangers. And in the household built on love there is always, too, the element of secrecy. There are things known to its members that no one else knows, the little secrets of the child, the ribbon in the drawer that chronicles the girl's first foolish love, the schoolboy letter with its stain of tears; things slight in themselves, occasions of laughter or brief sorrow, the little petulancies of a child's temper, the difficult confessions of a child's regret, the merry jests of happy hours; and the very essence of household intercourse is that these things make a bond of secret knowledge, something which lies behind all words, and colours all words, and exists for us alone. God's Household is such a household—*thy Father in heaven.* He encourages us to speak freely to Him in prayer: "in *everything* by prayer and supplication make your requests known unto God." He would rather that we spoke foolishly to Him, than that we framed our lips to the false rectitude of conceal- ment and reticence, for such reticence be- tokens lack of love and confidence. Don't pretend to God—there is no need—He knows everything. He asks only that you shall be natural, and He is better pleased with the most foolish thing you may say to Him in perfect trustfulness, than the most proper thing that really covers your distrust of Him. Bring Him smiles as well as tears; make Him so dear an intimate that your natural self moves with perfect freedom in His presence.

For, in its last analysis, prayer is *inti- macy* with God; it is the child's unembar- rassed conversation with his Father.

VIII

AND now let me return to the title of this little book, and ask why it is that prayer has become a Forgotten Secret? In one sense, of course, it is not forgotten; there are multitudes who know the secret, and perhaps far more than we suppose. But in two directions it is very evident that prayer has been forgotten, and the first of these is seen in the general organization of the church. Let any one be at pains to study the hand-book of any energetic church, and he will be at once aware of the small part which prayer plays in its scheme of life. For he will discover numerous records of clubs, and societies, and associations, ministering to the intellectual or social needs of the congregation, or serving as the vehicles of its benevolence, but he will often find no meeting that exists for prayer and prayer alone. Even in the common system of our public worship prayer has but a subordinate place. The actual time allotted to music often exceeds that allotted to prayer, and in most forms of Protestant worship the sermon is the one attraction. Yet there can be little doubt that in the earliest forms of Christian organization prayer occupied the chief place. Such instruction as was given was brief and informal. On the rare occasion of an apostolic visit there was the deliberate exposition of Christian truth, but the ordinary meeting of the people was for prayer and mutual encouragement. Cannot we revive the ancient practice? Would it not be an experiment worth making for some great church to discontinue for a whole month all its settled forms of worship, and invite its people to gather for the sole exercise of prayer?

We have seen for ourselves what has happened in Wales. The greatest revival in our generation, in the course of which eighty thousand people have publicly confessed Christ, has found its sole dynamic in prayer. There has been little preaching, neither elaborate music nor eloquent appeals, and no organization of effort, but there has been abundant praying. In one instance known to me, a simple farmer and his wife unlocked the door of a humble chapel on a lonely hillside, and themselves began to pray for their neighbours by name, until in one fortnight, drawn by an invisible compulsion, more than fifty persons so prayed for came to this unadvertised meeting, and yielded themselves to Christ. And this story is typical of the whole Welsh revival, which may be justly described as a rediscovery of the dynamic efficacy of prayer. So then the secret is not only open but thoroughly attested. Nothing proved by science is more plainly verified than that prayer is the supreme dynamic of the church. Is not the deduction obvious, that when the church returns to the practice of prayer, as the supreme expression of its life, it will at once rediscover the secret of conquest, which is often conspicuously absent in the best organized revival? We cannot really organize a revival, but we can organize ourselves.

As it has been with the church, so it has been with the individual Christian. He has been repleted with instruction, preached to so long and so often that he has become sermon-saturated, spurred to all sorts of semi-secular activities under the sanction of the church, but the one thing he has not been taught to do is to pray. He has learned all about the publicities of religion, but nothing of its secrecies. Sometimes in the desert I have come upon an empty spoliated temple, open to the four winds of heaven, through whose broken door the desert sand has drifted. No Vandal has been there, indeed, to overturn the altar, or inscribe his sacrilegious scorn upon the walls; but equally pitiful to me has seemed the drifted sand, the broken door, the silent long advance of the outward world into the shrine built for privacy. So, in the hearts of many good men, though no open desecration is discoverable, no stain of polluting orgies or ruin wrought by evil flame, yet there is the drift of worldliness, and of worldliness that takes a half religious form. We have to guard against the desert sand as well as the Vandal—it may prove more fatal. We have to beware of the spurious zeal which makes a business of the church, and invites the world to occupy the temple in the name of Christ. There is a kind of man, all too common in the church, who, in contributing to it his skilled business efficiency, which no doubt is needed, gradually comes to think, and makes others think, that the church itself is a kind of business. He can be cogent and convincing in a question of finance, but who ever heard him pray? He will manifest a splendid diligence on questions of secular detail, but who does not feel that the spiritual wave that thrills and softens many humbler hearts breaks on him in vain? So that with all his utilities, such a man is rather a hindrance to the church than a help; and his heart, long ignorant of the privacies of prayer, is drifted up with the dust and grit of the market-place. It is this man, of all men, who needs to be redeemed, both for the sake of his own good qualities, and the real value of those qualities to the church. And the redemption will only come by the reinstatement of prayer in his life, by its discovery, or rediscovery.

It is the secularization of the church which is the real source of all its barrenness, its ineptitude, its failure to attract men and mould society. For ordinary men, whatever we may say, and say truly, about the willful materialism of their lives, nevertheless have enough of right instinct to recognize the church as the one supreme spiritual force upon the earth, spiritual by origin, by history, and by profession; and when they see a spiritual institution willfully exchanging spiritual for secular methods of success, they naturally regard it with aversion or contempt. The ordinary man, also, if he be fairly educated, knows enough of the Gospels to be perfectly aware that the modern church in no way resembles that company of wise and simple souls whom Jesus gathered round Him in His earthly ministry. It is clear enough to the reader of the Gospels that Jesus founded no church in our sense of the term; He was content to gather round Him men and women of humble lives, whose sense of the unseen was so strong that they passed their time in prayer and good works, scorned riches and felt no shame in poverty, had neither a formal creed nor a binding scheme of worship, and were so sure of the spiritual efficacy which dwelt in their Master's word and example that they did not think it worth their while to use the wisdom of the world to make His kingdom known. Is it because we have no longer any real faith in this efficacy of the Master's word and example, that we have discarded our spiritual weapons for temporal ones, made it evident that the things upon which we rely for success are not faith and prayer, not the compulsion of truth and love, but rather such attractions as may lie in human eloquence, elaborate music, the solicitations of social advantage, and other things which are as indubitable products of wealth as the mansion of the millionaire and the fastidious elaboration of his luxury? The shrewd observer is not slow to draw this conclusion. The contrast between the methods of Jesus and the methods of the modern church is too glaring to be missed. The motto of Jesus is, "My kingdom is not of this world"; the motto of His church to-day appears to be, "My kingdom is the kingdom of this world, and my methods are the methods of the world, for in no other have I any confidence."

Even though it be granted that, by mere pressure of self-preservation, the original and simple society of Jesus was bound to organize itself, yet there is no reason why its primal elements should have perished in the process. Nor have they ever perished wholly, for after all there is a certain indestructible spiritual element in the church. That element, like a smothered fire, has continually sprung up in vital flame, in the unlikeliest ways and places; in the heart of a Francis of Assisi, in the zeal of the Lollards, in the enthusiasm of Wesley, in the tender passion of a Catherine of Siena, and a Catherine Booth. And therein lies our lesson; for whenever and wherever the spiritual element has regained ascendancy in the church, it has been the signal of immediate conquest. Men do not really desire the meretricious substitutes we offer them in the name of Christ; neither the ritual splendour, nor the seduction of art and music, nor the attractions of the social club; to the man spiritually hungry, as most men are, these things are the bitter gift of stones instead of bread. But the hungry man comes where the bread is, and the frozen man where the fire is. It is little after all that the world asks of us; it is simply that we shall give that which it is in our power to give, the impulse to man's latent spirituality; that we should show ourselves possessed of that which we boast is our sole prerogative, the spiritual dynamic which redeems the soul. To whomsoever this secret of the soul's dynamic is known men will gather, and in the long run they will gather to no one else. Let the church return to the life of prayer, and give proof that she is willing to trust to spiritual means alone for her success, and in the same hour the era of enduring conquest will begin.

If I venture thus to speak strongly of the main defect in modern Christianity, it is not in any spirit of censoriousness, and still less of superiority; I do but record a conclusion forced upon me by experience and observation. I am the friend and advocate of all that goes by the name of "the institutional church." It has always been my aim to build up around the church every sort of society and organization which can serve the social needs of the people, conserve their physical well-being, direct and stimulate their intellectual life, and thus fulfill the wide conception of a Christian manhood. But I have learned by disillusion and disappointment how little the most excellent series of institutions associated with a church may help its spiritual life; how apt they are to become secular in temper, with but the faintest and most fugitive relation to the things of the soul; and, what is much more disastrous, how often they usurp the function of the spiritual or tend towards its suppression. When this happens they become a menace to the church rather than a source of strength. The superficies is extended, but the centre suffers. The emphasis of life is put upon things outward instead of things inward. And what shall compensate us if the shrine and the altar are neglected? How can we justify our existence if we offer men nothing more than they can obtain without our aid from many other sources, and withhold from them that very bread of life which Christ has entrusted to our custody? They who drink of the water of a secularized Christianity indeed thirst again; only from the spiritual Rock flows that water of which, when a man drinks, he thirsts no more.

Could we gather a consensus of confession from those whose words are best worth heeding in all the churches, it would be the barrenness of definite result which would make that confession significant. With all our eager toil, all our organized efficiency, all our efforts to attract, how scanty the result, how incommensurable the harvest with the sowing! Is it possible that we do not perceive the real cause of our misfortune and defeat? For that cause is lucid to all but ourselves; barrenness of spiritual result is the punishment of prayerlessness; it is its appointed Nemesis. I remember once, when visiting at a country house in the hottest period of the year, being surprised by the perfume of flowers that filled my bedroom in the early morning, until rising almost with the sun one morning, I discovered the reason. It was a very simple reason, nothing more than this, that with the first light the gardener was busy watering the flowers beneath my window, and from those watered flowers came the fragrance that filled my room with sweetness. There are lives also, that, exposed to the hottest sun of daily toil, possess the secret of freshness and perfume and are unwithered, because they are kept watered with the living water that flows from the throne of God and of the Lamb. "He maketh me to lie down in green pastures, and beside still waters." Prayer is the soul's pasture and the soul's dew, and he who prays much is as "a tree planted by the rivers of water, whose leaf shall not wither."

It was because Jesus dwelt thus in the secret places of prayer that His life possessed that freshness of spiritual grace which time has not withered, and that repose and infinite tranquillity, the very contemplation of which overcomes our souls with wonder. It is in the renewed and deeper study of that life; in the hours of loneliness and separation when, in the intervals of public work, I have had no one to talk with but God; in the episodes of that public work itself, when again and again it has happened that sons, and brothers, and husbands in distant cities have yielded to the silent compulsions of God's grace in the very hour when friends were praying for them; it is in these things that there has come to me, in my own experience, the rediscovery of this Forgotten Secret of prayer. To him who has found the secret, life takes a new significance, and faith receives a new sanction. We have but to make the experiment of prayer to discover its eternal efficacy. And the way of that experiment is so simple that a child may understand it:

"BUT THOU, WHEN THOU PRAYEST, ENTER INTO THY CLOSET, AND WHEN

THOU HAST SHUT THY DOOR, PRAY TO THY FATHER WHICH IS IN SECRET ; AND THY FATHER WHICH SEETH IN SECRET SHALL REWARD THEE OPENLY."

CPSIA information can be obtained
at www.ICGtesting.com
Printed in the USA
BVHW040916211218
536170BV00015B/492/P

9 781331 865995